EASY KEYBOARD
PIECES FOR KIDS

30 Simple Keyboard Pieces for Beginners

ISBN: 9798602928839

CONTENTS

3   Mary Had a Little Lamb / Hot Cross Buns

4   Little Bird

5   Go and Tell Aunt Dinah / Clown Dance

6   Aura Lee

7   Ten Little Indians / Kum Ba Yah

8   Old Macdonald Had a Farm

9   Ode to Joy / Enroulez le Fils

10   Twinkle, Twinkle Little Star

11   Au Clair de la Lune

12   Jingle Bells

13   London Bridge / Skip to My Lou

14   Michael Row the Boat Ashore / Frère Jacques

15   What Shall we Do with the Drunken Sailor

16   Happy Birthday to You / While Shepherds Watched

17   For He's a Jolly Good Fellow

18   Lavender's Blue / Scarborough Fair

19   My Bonnie Lies Over the Ocean

20   She'll be Comin' Round the Mountain

21   Good King Wenceslas

22   Amazing Grace

23   Greensleeves

24   Away in a Manger

Introduction

This collection of easy tunes for keyboard or piano is perfect for children and older beginners. The initial tunes use only 3 - 5 different notes but by the end of the book the tunes range to over an octave with some sharps and flats also being used.

For those who are still learning to read the music and remember which note is which the following reference chart shows how to find all of the notes used in this book:

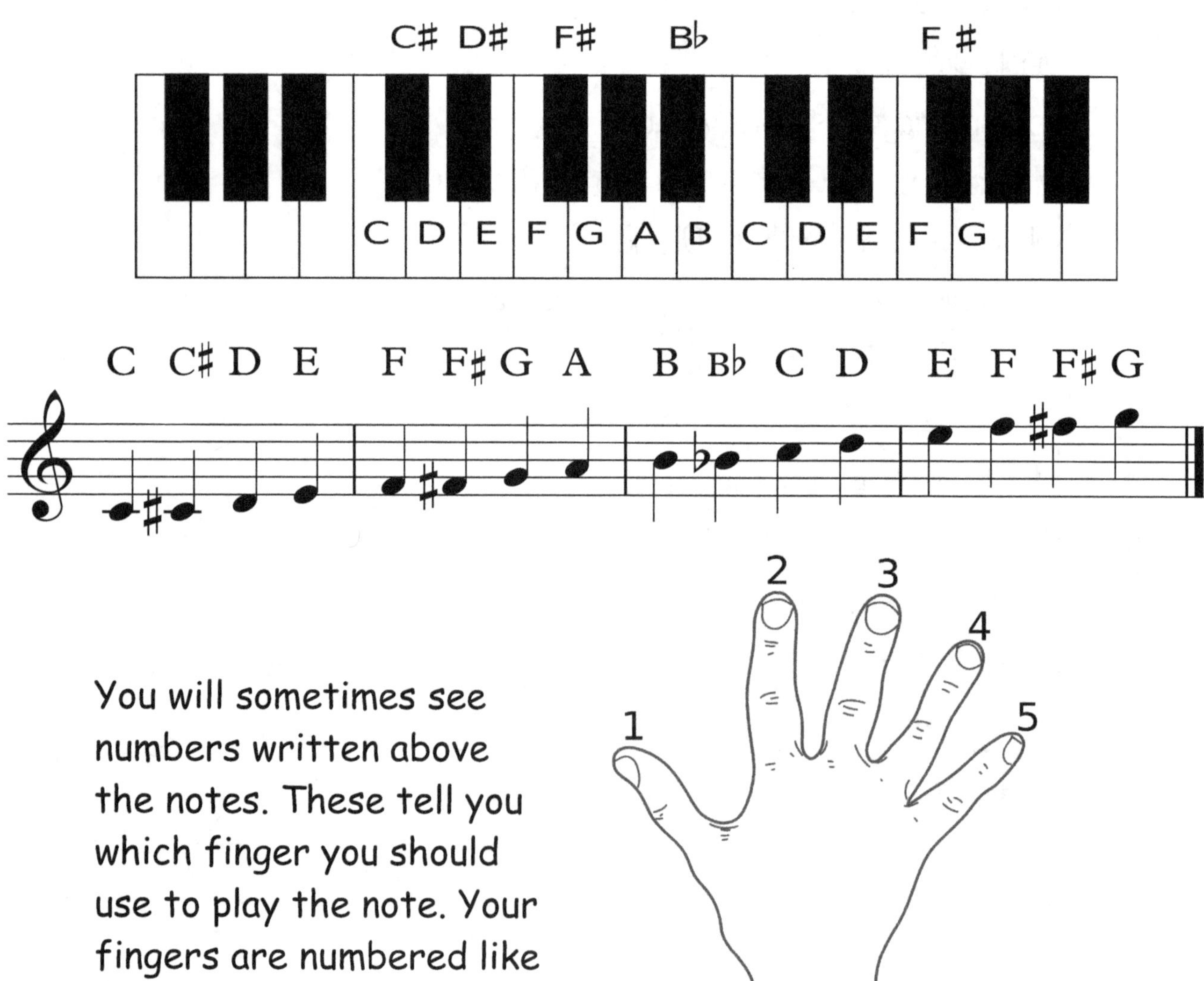

You will sometimes see numbers written above the notes. These tell you which finger you should use to play the note. Your fingers are numbered like this:

Mary Had a Little Lamb

3 2 1 2 3 2 3 5
E D C D E E E D D D E G G
Ma-ry had a li-ttle lamb, li-ttle lamb, li-ttle lamb,

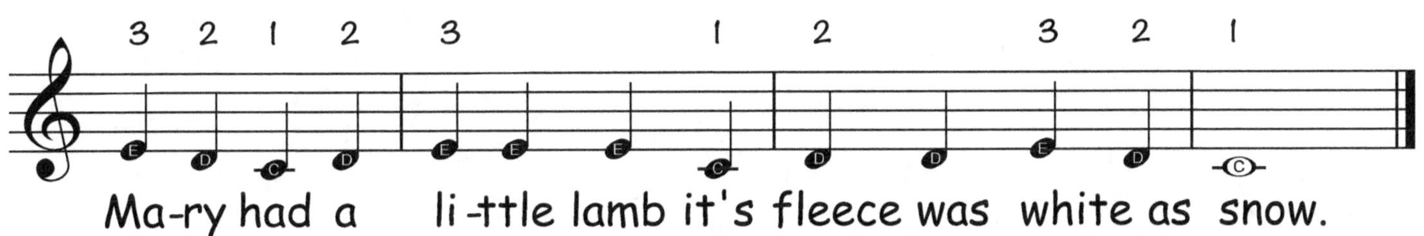

3 2 1 2 3 1 2 3 2 1
E D C D E E E C D D E D C
Ma-ry had a li-ttle lamb it's fleece was white as snow.

Hot Cross Buns

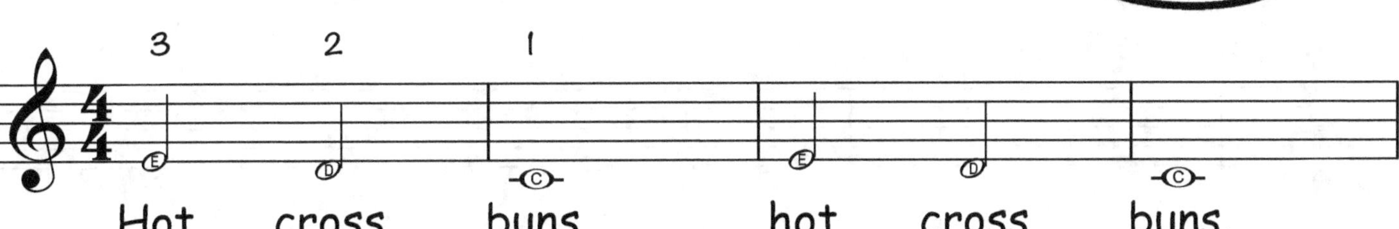

3 2 1
E D C E D C
Hot cross buns, hot cross buns.

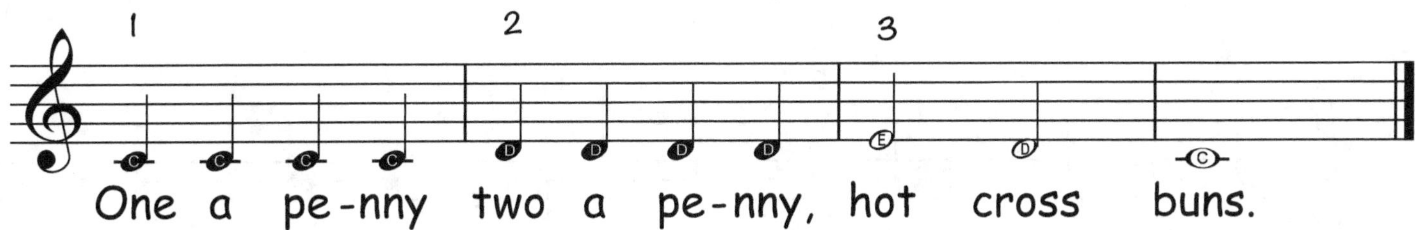

1 2 3
C C C C D D D D E D C
One a pe-nny two a pe-nny, hot cross buns.

Little Bird

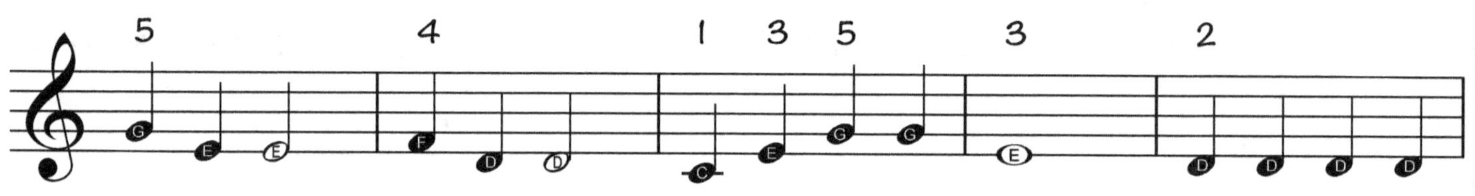

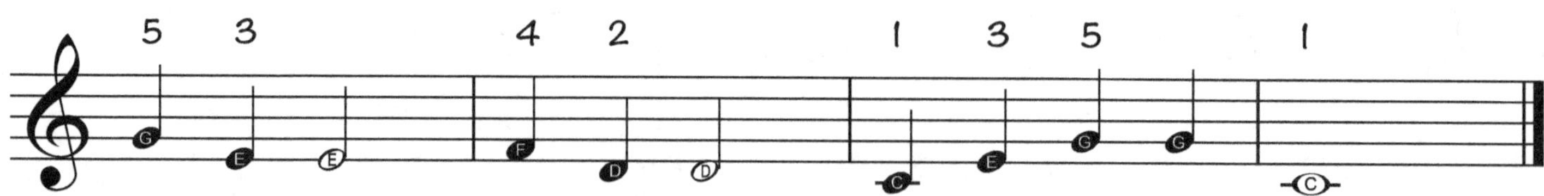

Go and Tell Aunt Dinah

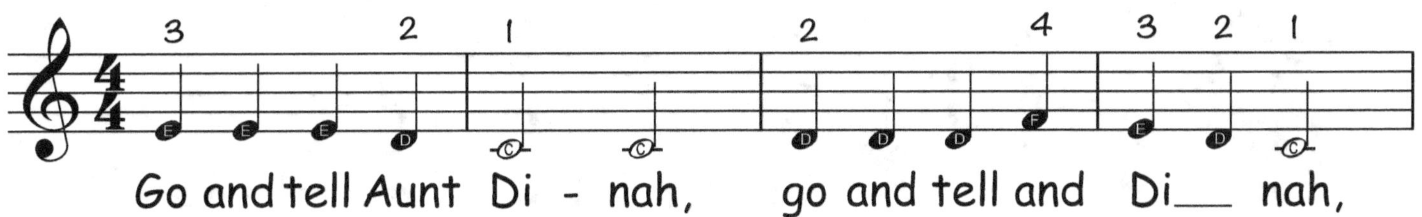

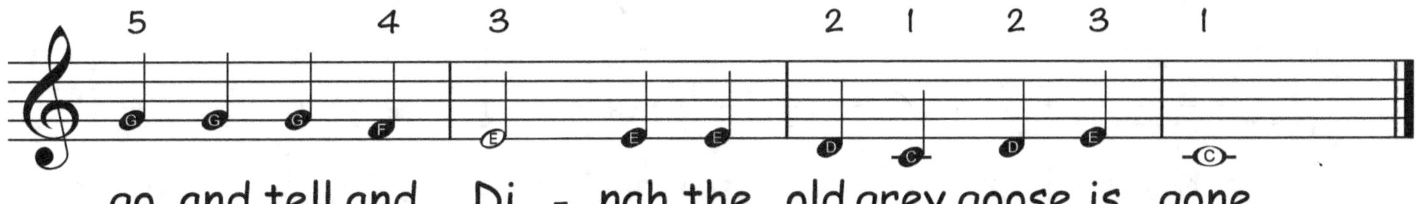

Clown Dance

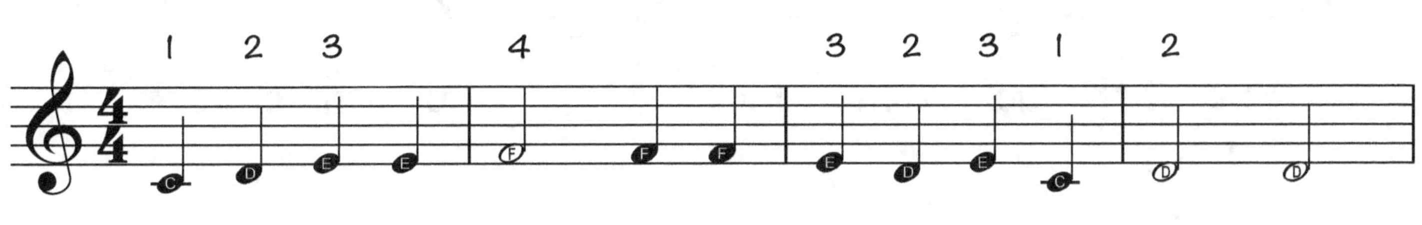

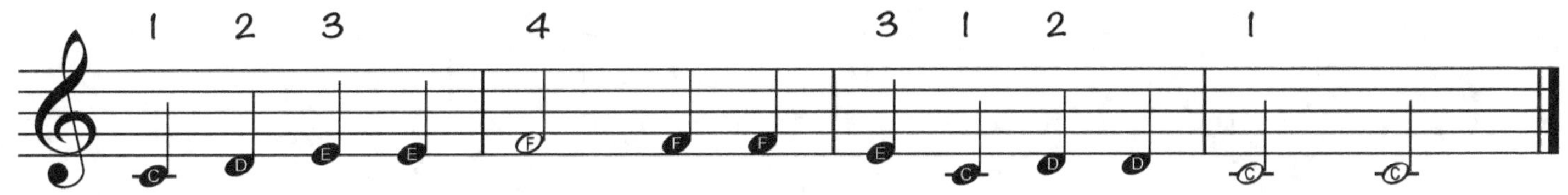

Aura Lee

As   the   black-bird   in   the   spring,

on the wi-llow tree,   sat and rocked I heard him sing,

sing of Au -ra   Lee.   Aur-a Lee,   Aur-a Lee,
maid with gol - den   hair,   sun -shine came   a -

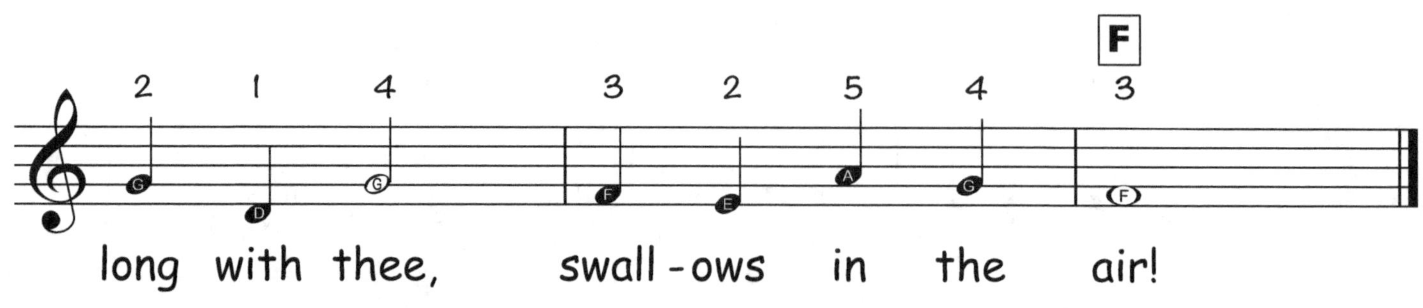
long with thee,   swall-ows   in   the   air!

Ten Little Indians

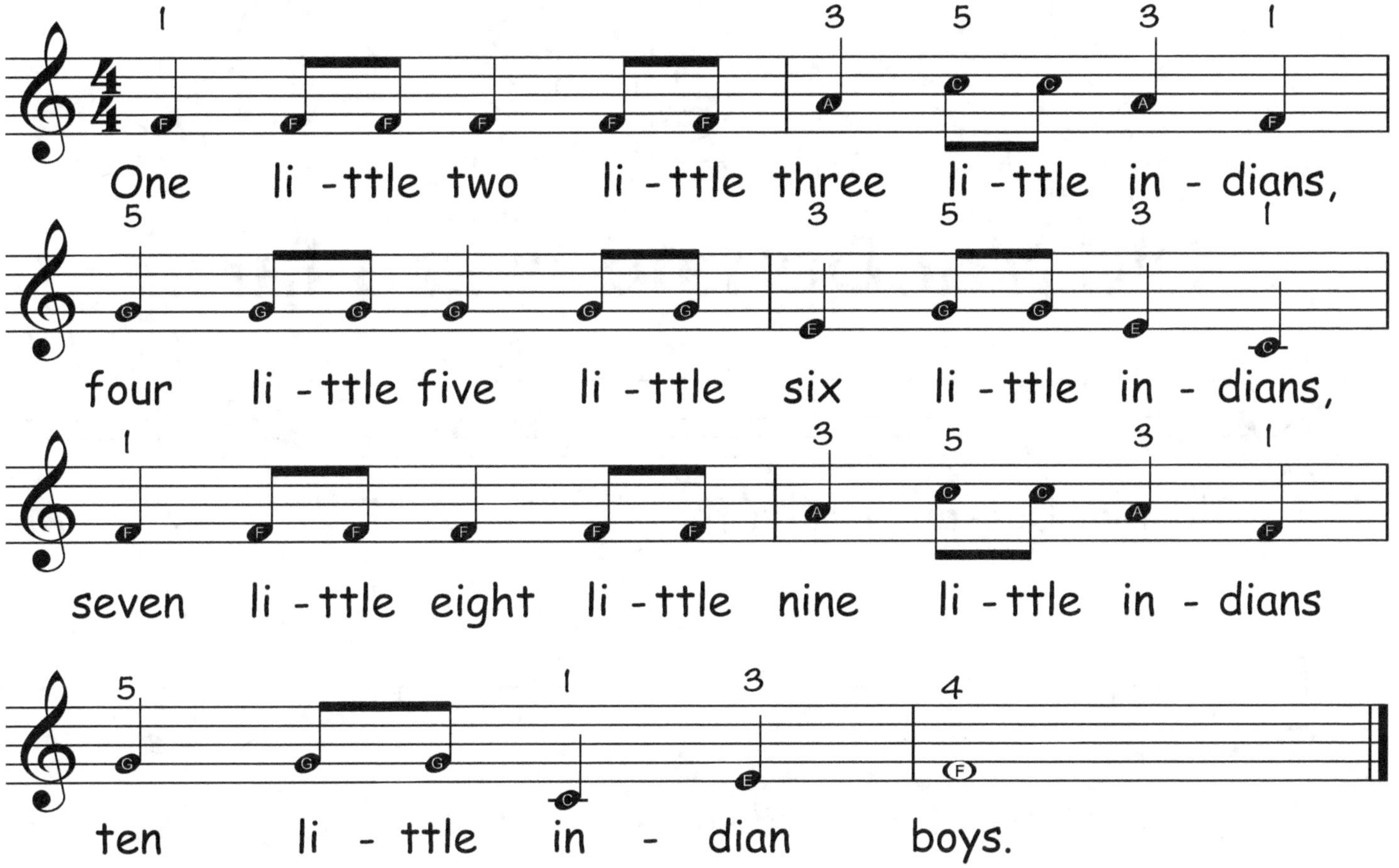

One li -ttle two li -ttle three li -ttle in - dians,
four li -ttle five li -ttle six li -ttle in - dians,
seven li -ttle eight li -ttle nine li -ttle in - dians
ten li - ttle in - dian boys.

Kum Ba Yah

Kum ba ya my lord, kum ba yah____ Kum ba
ya my lord kum ba yah____ kum ba yah my lord
kum ba yah____ Oh lord kum bah ya.

Old MacDonald had a farm

Old Mac Don-ald had a farm,   E I E I O.   And

on that farm he   had some ducks,   E I E I

O.   With a quack quack here,   quack quack there,

here a quack, there a quack,   eve-ry where a quack quack.

Old Mac Don-ald had a farm.   E I E I O.

Ode to Joy

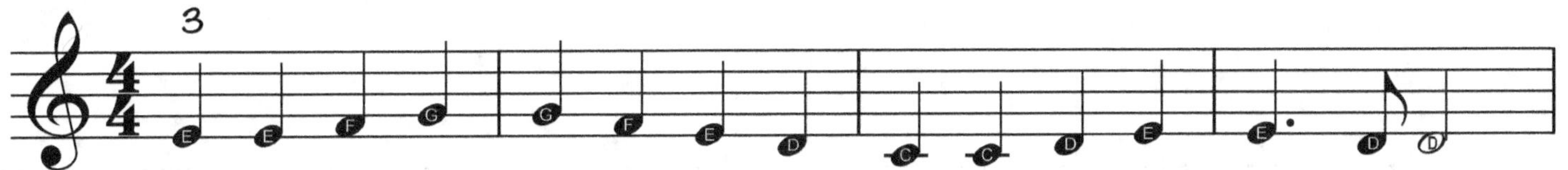

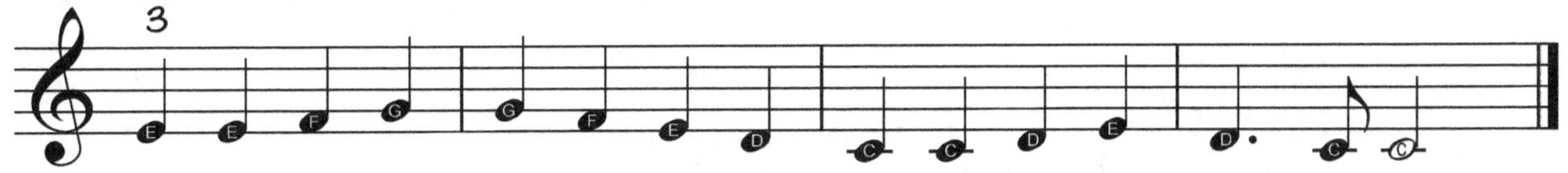

Enroulez le Fils

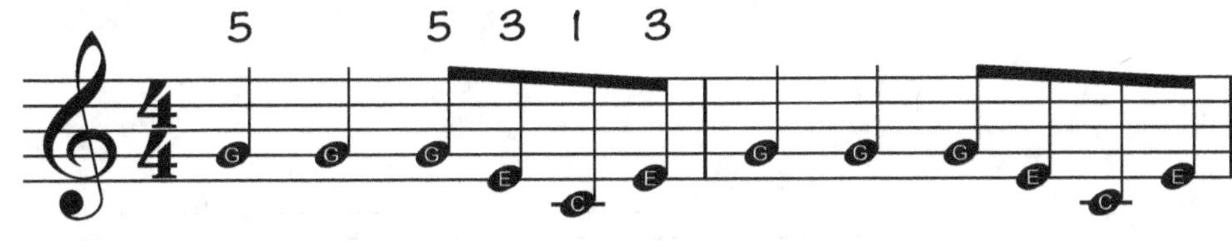

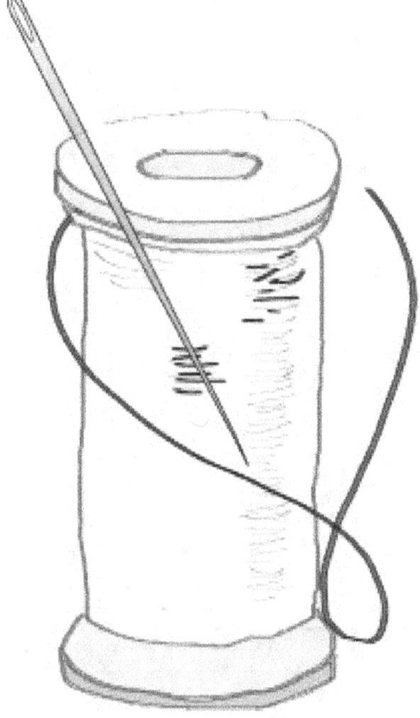

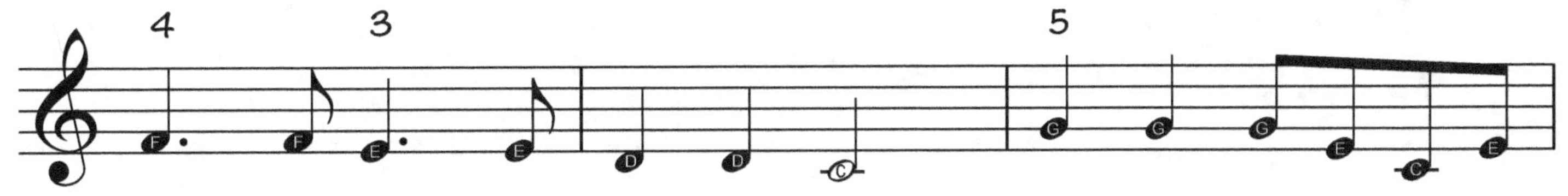

Twinkle Twinkle Little Star

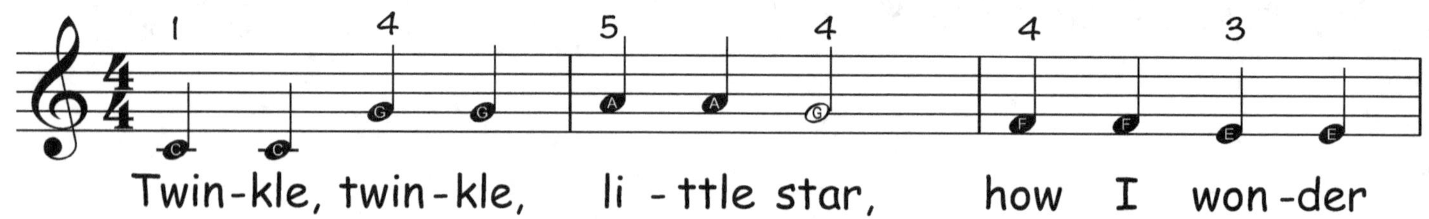
1   4   5   4   4   3
C   C   G   G   A   A   G   F   F   E   E
Twin-kle, twin-kle, li -ttle star,   how I   won-der

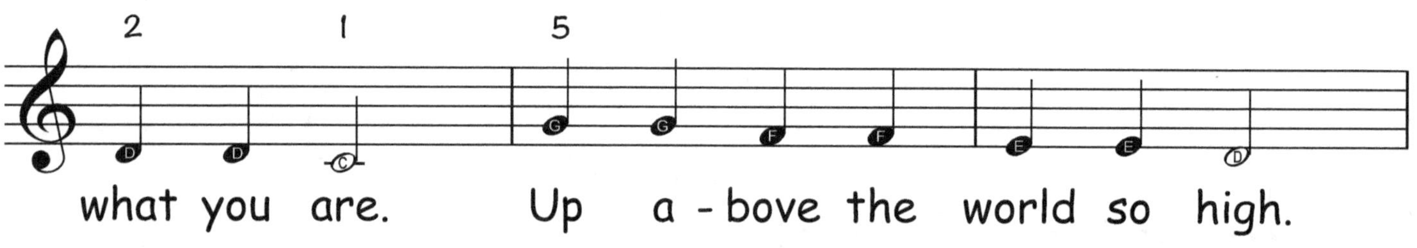
2   1   5
D   D   C   G   G   F   F   E   E   D
what you are.   Up   a -bove the world so high.

1   4
G   G   F   F   E   E   D   C   C   G   G
Like a   dia-mond in   the sky.   Twin-kle, twin-kle

5   4   4
A   A   G   F   F   E   E   D   D   C
li -ttle star,   how I   won-der what you are.

Au Clair de la Lune

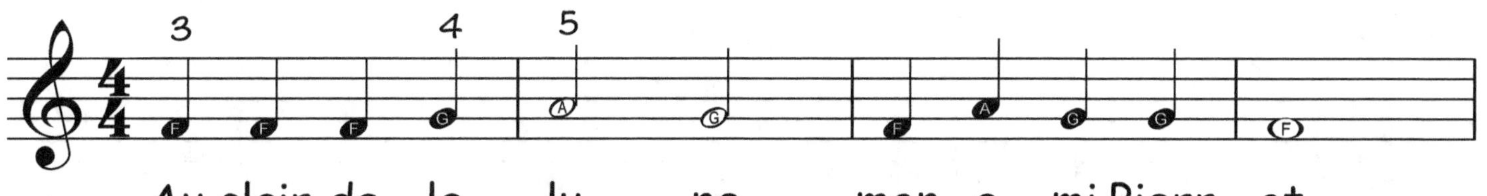

Au clair de la lu - ne, mon a - mi Pierr - ot.

Au clair de la lu - ne, mon a - mi Pierr - ot.

Ma chan - delle est mor - te, Je n'ai plus de feu.

Ouv - re moi ta por - te, pour l'am - our de Dieu!

Jingle Bells

3   3 5 1 2 3
Jin-gle bells,   jin-gle bells,   jin-gle all   the way,

4   2   5
Oh what fun it   is to ride in a once horse o-pen   sleigh_

3
Jin-gle bells,   jin-gle bells,   jin-gle all   the way,

4   4 3   5   4 2 1
Oh what fun it   is to ride in a one horse o-pen   sleigh!

London Bridge is Falling Down

Lon - don bridge is fa -lling down, fa -lling down,
fa - lling down. Lon - don bridge is
fa - lling down, my fair la - dy.

Skip to My Lou

Choose your part-ners skip to my Lou, choose your part-ners
skip to my Lou, choose your part - ners
skip to my Lou, skip to my Lou my dar - lin'.

Michael Row the Boat Ashore

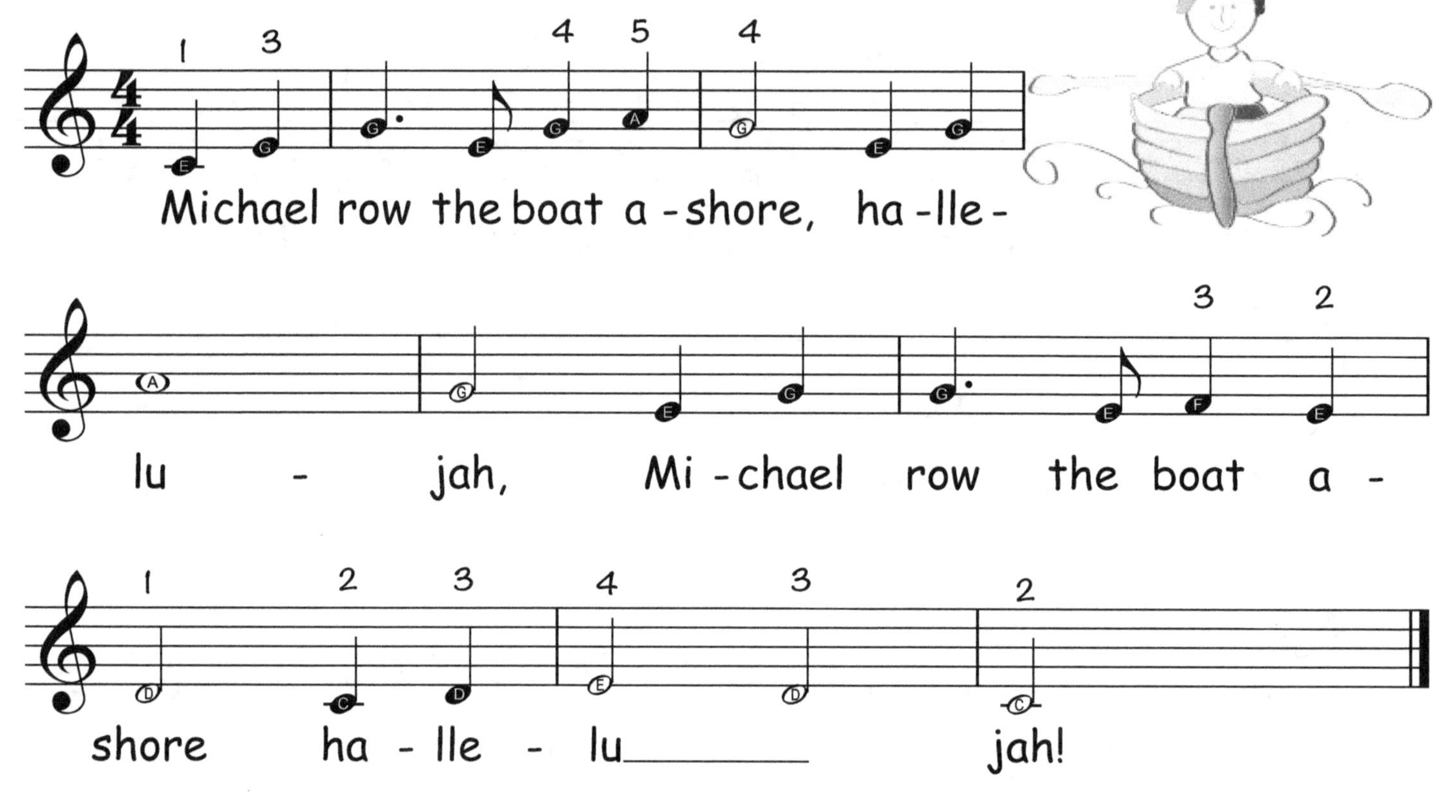
Michael row the boat a -shore, ha -lle-
lu - jah, Mi -chael row the boat a -
shore ha - lle - lu________ jah!

Frère Jacques

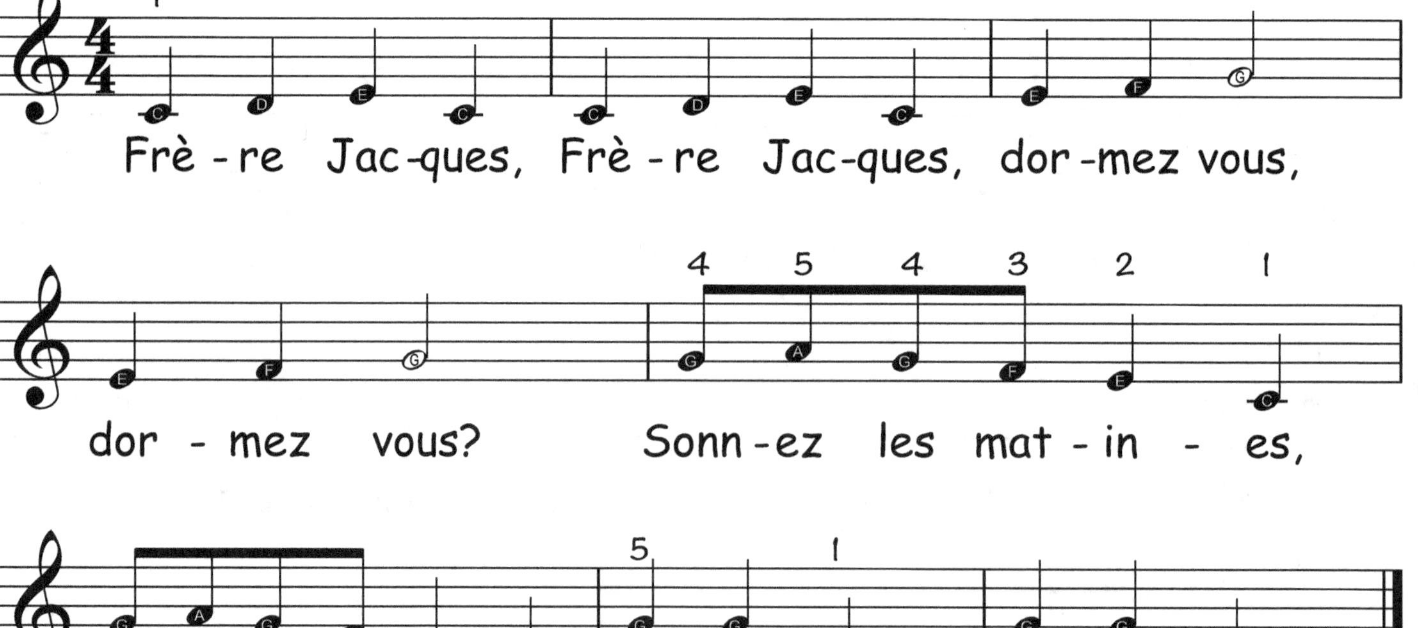
Frè -re Jac-ques, Frè -re Jac-ques, dor -mez vous,
dor - mez vous? Sonn -ez les mat -in - es,
sonn ez les mat-in - es, ding dang dong, ding dang dong!

What shall we do with the drunken sailor?

What shall we do with the drunk - en sail - or,
what shall we do with the drunk - en sail - or,
what shall we do with the drunk - en sail - or

earl - y in the morn - ing? Hoo - ray
up she ris - es, hoo - ray up she ri - ses, hoo - ray
up she ri - ses earl - y in the morn - ing.

Happy birthday to you!

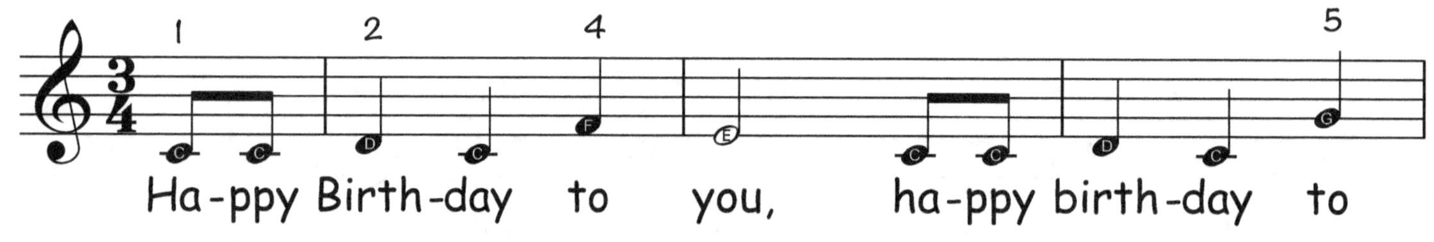
Ha-ppy Birth-day to you, ha-ppy birth-day to

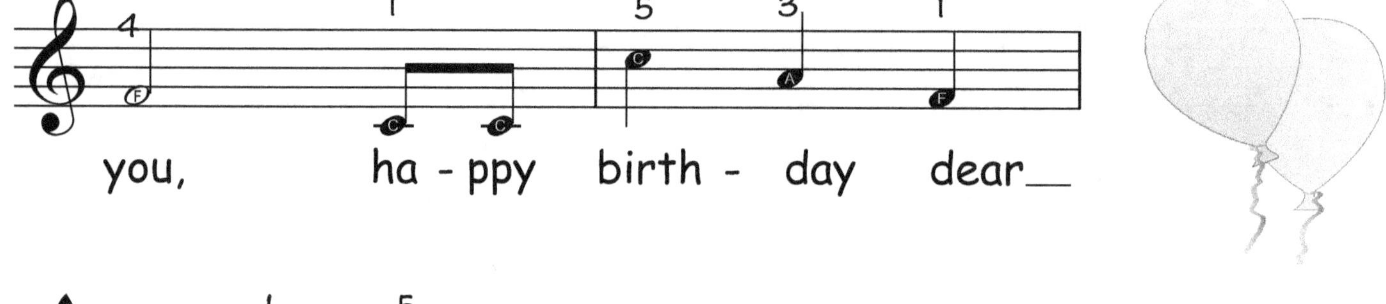
you, ha-ppy birth-day dear___

___________ Ha-ppy birth-day to you!

While shepherds watched

While shep-herds watched their flocks by night all
seat-ed on the ground, the an-gel of the

Lord came down and glo-ry shone a-round.

For He's a Jolly Good Fellow

For he's a jo-lly good fe - llow, for he's a
jo-lly good fe - llow, for he's a jo-lly good fe____
llow, and so say all of us. And so say
all of us, and so say all of us.
O, for he's a jo-lly good fe - llow, for he's a
jo-lly good fe - llow, for he's a jo-lly good fe____
llow and so say all of us____

Lavender's Blue

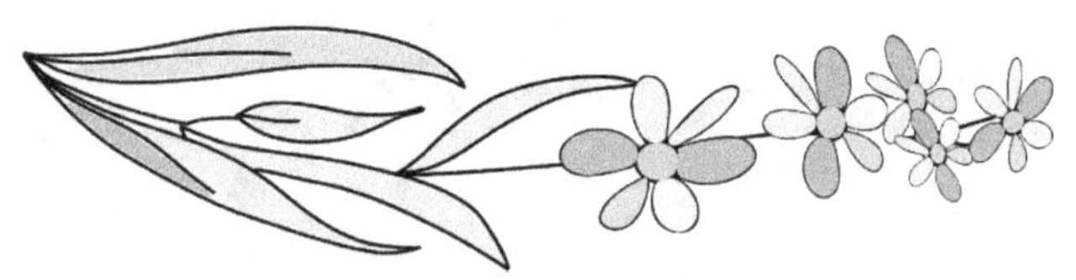

Lav - en -der's blue di -lly di -lly, lav - en -der's green.

When you are king di -lly di -lly I will be queen.

Scarborough Fair

Are you going to Scar-borough fair? Pars - ley, sage, rose

ma -ry and thyme. Re -mem - ber me to one who lives

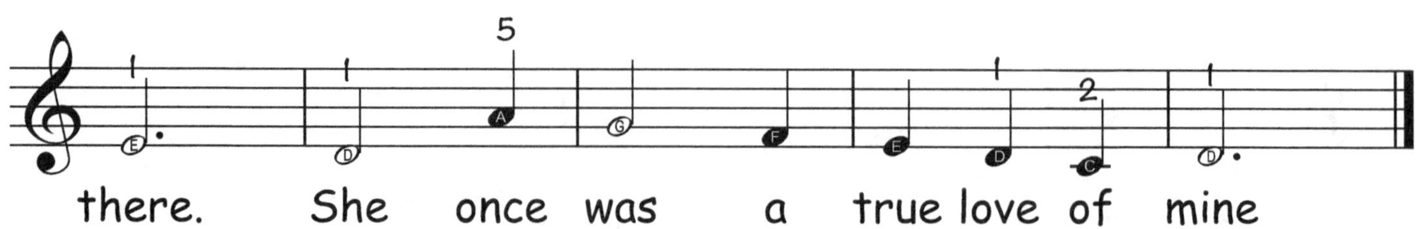

there. She once was a true love of mine

My Bonnie Lies Over the Ocean

My Bonn-ie lies o-ver the
o- cean,___ my Bonn-ie lies
o-ver the sea,___ my Bonnie lies o-ver the o- cean,
o bring back my Bonnie to me.___ Bring
back, bring back, O bring back my Bonnie to me to
me. Bring back, bring back O
bring back my Bonn-ie to me.___

She'll be Comin' Round the Mountain

She'll be com-in' round the moun-tain when she comes, she'll be

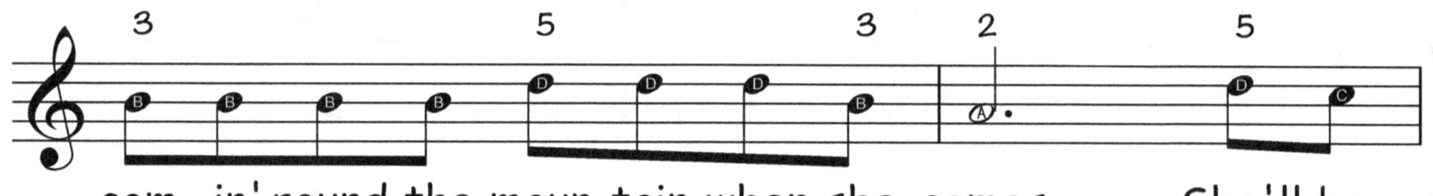
com-in' round the moun-tain when she comes.   She'll be

com in' round the moun-tain,   com in' round the moun-tain,

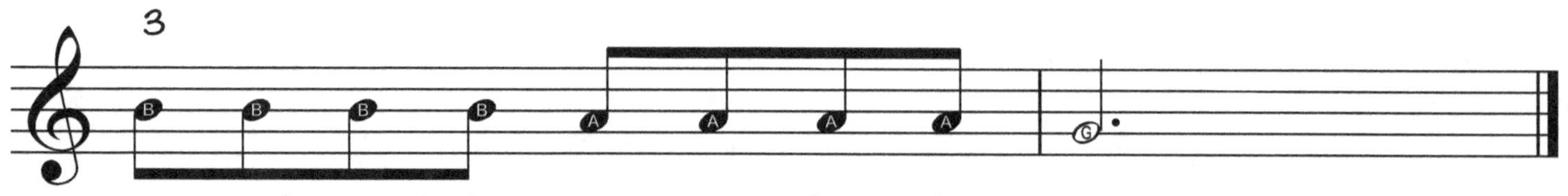
com-in' round the moun-tain when she comes.

Good King Wenceslas

Good King Wen-ces-las looked out,
on the feast of Ste - phen. When the snow lay
round a - bout, deep and crisp and e - ven.
Bright-ly shone the moon that night, though the frost was
cru - el, when a poor man came in sight,
gath -ring win - ter fu________ el.

Amazing Grace

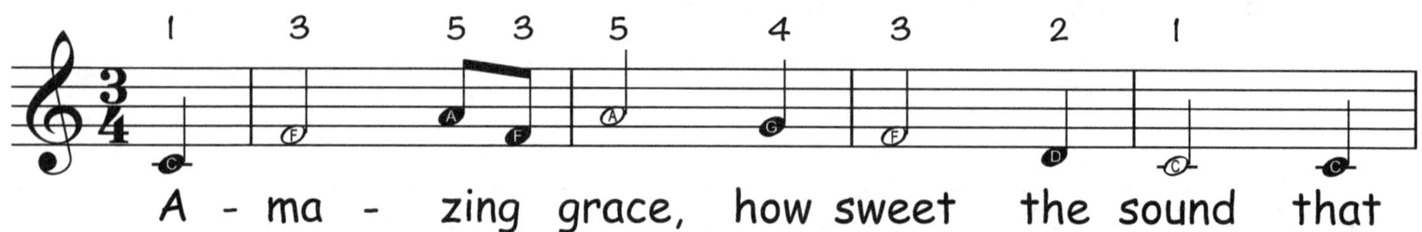

A - ma - zing grace, how sweet the sound that

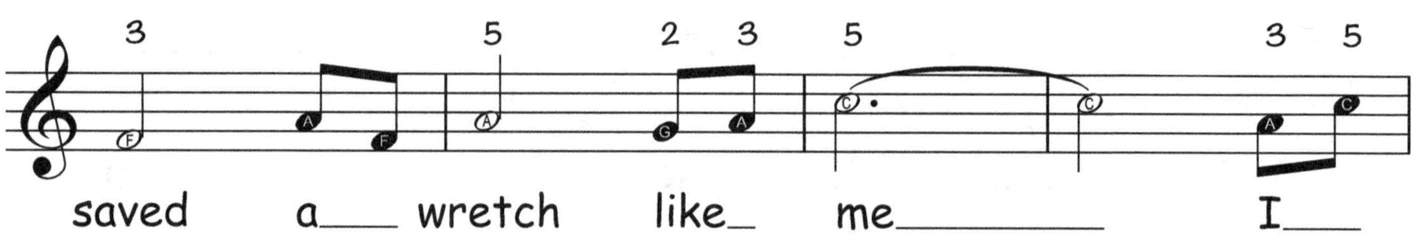

saved a__ wretch like_ me________ I__

once was_ lost but now am found, was_

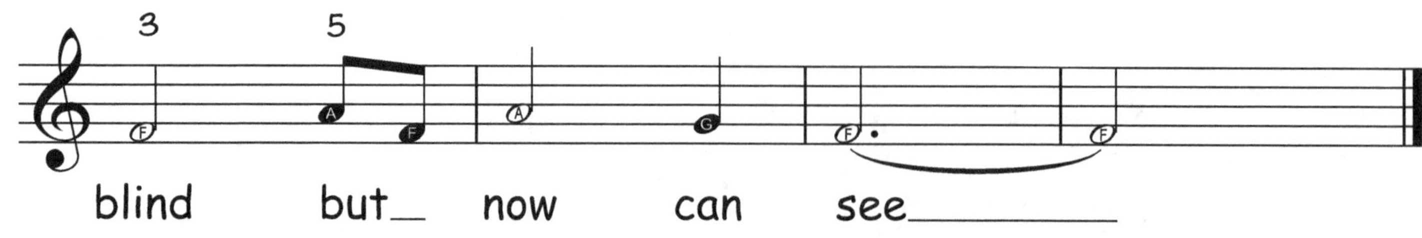

blind but_ now can see________

Greensleeves

A - las   my   love___ you   do   me

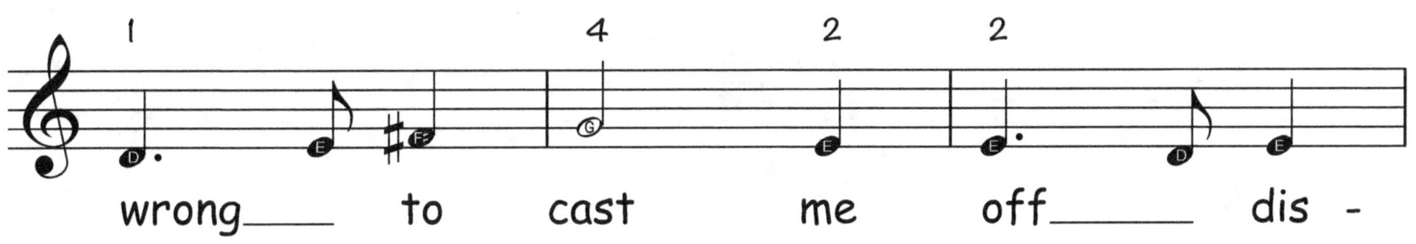
wrong___   to   cast   me   off_____   dis -

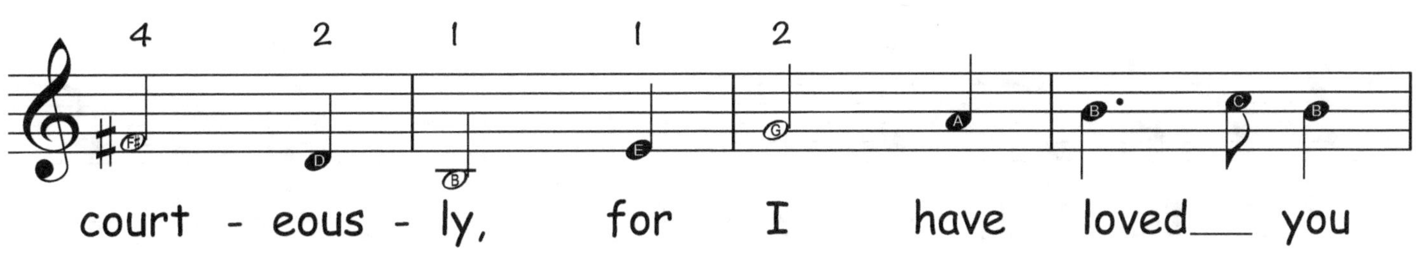
court - eous - ly,   for   I   have   loved___ you

well   and   long_____   de - light - ing

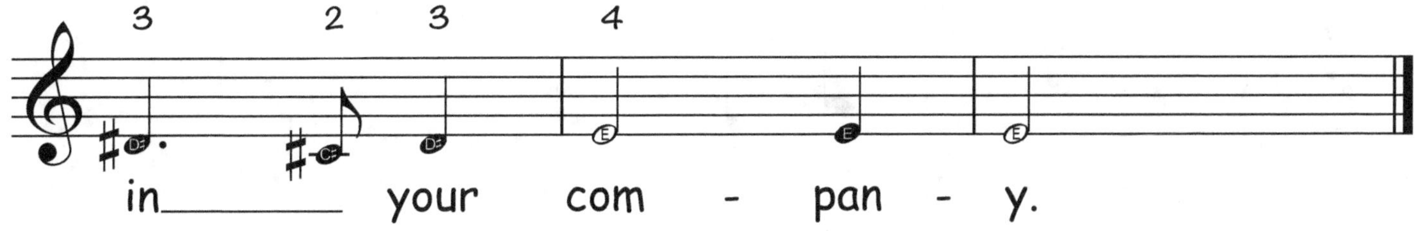
in_____   your   com - pan - y.

Away in a Manger

A - way in a__ manger no__
crib for a bed, the li -ttle lord

Je -sus laid_ down his sweet head. The stars in the_

bright sky looked down where he lay, the__

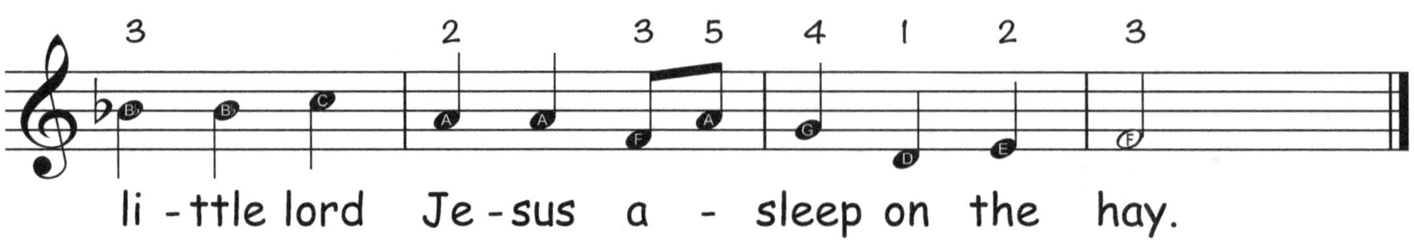

li -ttle lord Je -sus a - sleep on the hay.